Cheapskate's Little Instr

by
Mary Hunt

Trade Life Books
Tulsa, Oklahoma

2nd Printing

Cheapskate's Little Instruction Book
ISBN 1-57757-758-2
Copyright © 2000 by Mary Hunt
Published by Trade Life Books
P.O. Box 55325
Tulsa, OK 74155

Cover illustration by Anderson Thomas Design

Cover design by Randall Miller Design, Inc.

Introduction

Tiptionary, published in 1997 by Broadman & Holman, is "a grand smorgasbord loaded with every kind of delicacy you can possibly imagine—even some things you can't." In contrast, the *Cheapskate's Little Instruction Book*, is the deli version. We've taken the most intriguing and useful tips, hints, and suggestions from *Tiptionary* to create this little portable to help you save time, money, and aspirin.

Need a quick recipe for kids' face paint? It's in here. How about a clever way to figure out how many whole chickens it takes to make a cup of chopped chicken (no kidding). Then there's the best way to pick out a fresh fish at the market (avoid the ones with cloudy eyes). There's something for everyone—from moms, to dads, and even kids.

So make yourself a tuna sandwich, pour a glass of iced tea, put up your slippered feet, and read about why you need to apply sunscreen to your dashboard (seriously).

FAMILY

CHEAPSKATE'S LITTLE INSTRUCTION BOOK

Astringent

Instead of purchasing an expensive brand-name astringent for use in your skin-care regimen, use witch hazel, an old standby that has been recommended by skin professionals for decades. It's available over the counter at any drugstore and performs equally well to any brand of astringent, no matter how expensive.

Boot stretch

If your boots are too snug, try this: Place a strong plastic bag (test first to make sure it is watertight) in the boot, and fill the bag with enough water to fill the cavity. Tie the bag closed, and place the whole thing in the freezer. As the water freezes it will expand and will stretch the boot at the same time. This technique works well for shoes, too.

Clothing swap

Arrange a clothing swap with friends. Ask everyone to bring at least five items in good condition that no longer fit, flatter, or meet their needs. One person's disaster could be another person's delight!

Consignment stores

Consignment shops are everywhere these days and are a wonderful source for previously owned clothing. These shops are many cuts above thrift stores and offer wonderful merchandise for a fraction of the original retail price. Look for specialty consignment stores just for kids. And don't think of yourself only as a buyer, but also a seller. Typically you will share fifty/fifty with the store's owner when your items sell. Call ahead to learn of the store's policies regarding the condition of garments they will accept and other guidelines.

Extraneous coupons

What do you do with all the coupons you can't use? Clip them neatly and categorize them with gifts in mind. For instance, for the next baby shower, make up a clever holder full of coupons for diapers, baby food, and other items for the new mom (make sure the coupons haven't expired). Provide a great coupon assortment for the newly married couple to assist them in stocking their pantry. Have a friend or relative with a pet? Enclose some good coupons for pet food or supplies in their next birthday card.

Face paint

Ingredients: one teaspoon cornstarch, one-half teaspoon water, one-half teaspoon cold cream, and food coloring. Mix first three ingredients, and blend well. Add food coloring a drop at a time until you get the color you want. With a small paintbrush, paint chubby little faces. Allow paint to dry. Remove with cold cream. Store paint in small covered containers.

Do impromptu video interviews of family members regarding the past year's experiences with the primary goal of capturing how your kids have grown in a one-year span. Each year, close the video with a shot of the entire family taken in the same spot.

Generic equivalents

Ask for generic prescriptions, which cost up to 50 percent less, yet by law must have the same chemical makeup and potency. Also, buy generic non-prescription pain medication. One brand-name ibuprofen costs about eight dollars for one hundred tablets, while the generic costs about two dollars for the same amount. Be sure to consult the pharmacist when in doubt.

Hair treatment

A typical hair salon will charge twenty-five to thirty-five dollars for a special treatment to remove a buildup of minerals, conditioners, sprays, mousses, and gels. Here's an inexpensive alternative one professional hairdresser uses on her own hair: Wash hair with a gentle shampoo, and rinse with cool water. Towel dry hair. Saturate hair with apple cider vinegar (not white vinegar because it's too harsh). Wrap hair in a plastic cap or plastic wrap, and heat with a blow dryer for ten to fifteen minutes. Rinse hair thoroughly, and shampoo again.

Health insurance

Never be without health insurance. High deductibles with low premiums are recommended if you are and plan to remain healthy, because this type of coverage is for the big catastrophic events. One uninsured catastrophic illness or accident could wipe out everything for which you have saved and planned.

Just like "being there"

Make a videotape of your kids. Grandparents, for instance, would love to see them in action, especially if they live some distance away. So instead of capturing a planned and posed session, record the everyday events: bike riding, a live tooth-development demonstration, piano practice, or just getting ready for bed. Merry Christmas Grandma and Grandpa!

Kids' medications

Don't use tableware spoons when giving medicine to a child. Teaspoons and tablespoons in your silverware drawer may not hold the correct amount of liquid. A tableware spoon that's off by even one milliliter (0.0338 fluid ounce), could mean you're giving the child 20 percent more or less of the recommended dose of medicine. Use a proper measuring device, either one provided with the medicine or purchased separately, such as a measuring spoon, syringe, oral dropper, etc. You can ask the pharmacist for a complimentary calibrated measuring device for ease in dispensing liquid medications.

Learn while you drive

If you are average, you drive about fifteen thousand miles each year, which expressed in time equals about one college semester. Use that time spent in the car listening to books on tape or self-improvement tapes.

Low-cost spaying and neutering

An organization called Friends of Animals offers spaying and neutering at a reduced cost. They function like an HMO. You send them a check for twenty-five or fifty-nine dollars (depending on dog or cat, male or female), and they will send you a certificate that will cover the cost of the operation, hospitalization, and suture removal. You can take that certificate and your animal to one of the vets on their long list of choices in your area. For more information, Friends of Animals can be reached at 800-321-7387.

Move midweek

If you're moving, do it on a weekday. Fees can be as much as 50 percent higher on the weekend. Pack everything yourself and save at least 10 percent. Most movers provide cartons.

Negatives in safekeeping

To save precious memories in the event of a future house fire or some other disaster that would destroy your family photograph collection, take some negatives from each year's pictures (not all of them because that would be too many), and put them in your safe-deposit box. Then, heaven forbid, should you endure a disaster and lose all of your photos, you can at least get some of them reprinted.

Pantyhose longevity

According to the Morton Salt™ Company, your pantyhose will last longer and be less prone to snagging and running if you perform this little longevity trick before you wear them for the first time: Mix two cups of salt with one gallon of water, and immerse panty hose in the solution. Soak for three hours. Rinse in cold water and drip dry. Apparently one of the properties of ordinary table salt is the ability to toughen fibers. This solution will work for broom bristles as well.

Photocopies

Before spending a lot of money for enlargements and reprints of color photographs, consider making color photocopies at your local stationer or quick-print shop. For example, an eight-by-ten-inch color-copy enlargement costs less than two dollars, instead of ten dollars or more for a color-print enlargement. Although the paper is not as sturdy, once a photocopy is framed or mounted it is very difficult to detect any difference. Framed photos make great gifts.

Play dough

In a large pot, combine three cups flour, one and a half cups salt, and six teaspoons cream of tartar. In a separate bowl, mix three cups cool water, three tablespoons vegetable oil, and food coloring of choice. Stir into large-pot mixture. Heat over medium heat, stirring constantly until mixture coagulates and begins to pull away from the sides of the pan, or for about five minutes. Turn onto a cutting board and allow to cool slightly. Knead until smooth and feels like play dough. Store in an airtight container.

Presidential greetings

Greeting cards and notes from the White House are available for the following: serious illnesses, eightieth (or beyond) birthday celebrations, fiftieth (or more) wedding anniversaries, birth announcements, and to Boy and Girl Scouts who have gone beyond the call of duty. Send the details of the greeting you are requesting to: White House, Greeting Office, Room 39, Washington, DC 20500, or call 202-456-2724.

Skin-care products

A reader asked a doctor friend what he learned during his dermatology rotation concerning expensive skin and facial cleansing products. He informed her that the best products are not the most expensive. Dermatologists recommend Dove™ or Lever 2000™ for cleansing and Lubriderm™ lotion for moisturizing. Both products are sold over the counter at any drug store and most grocery stores.

Shoe rotation

You've heard of rotating your car's tires to make them last longer, but how about rotating your footwear? Research shows that your feet produce about one half pint of water every day. If you wear a particular pair of shoes no more than once every three days, three pairs will hold up as long as four pairs worn more frequently. Shoes need at least forty-eight hours to rest, dry out, and resume their normal shape.

Get a big cardboard box and cut holes for a door and windows. Let the kids color the box. Help them draw flowers at the bottom, shutters on the windows, maybe curtains on the windows. The possibilities are limitless. Washer, dryer, or other large boxes are ideal.

"We missed you" photo

Photograph your family for the friends and family members who could not attend a special event or holiday gathering. Have your pictures developed at a place that offers a complimentary second set of prints, and send them out along with a note to tell your friends and family how much they were missed.

There are several things you can do to get that stubborn, sluggish, sticking metal zipper back into tip-top shape. Here are a few. Run the lead of an ordinary pencil along the metal zipper teeth to lubricate them. Or, with a cotton swab, apply a bit of lubricating spray such as WD-40™ to the teeth. Be careful to wipe away any excess so it won't soil the garment. Another solution is to rub the edge of a bar of soap or an old candle up and down the teeth and along both sides of the zipper.

FOOD

CHEAPSKATE'S LITTLE INSTRUCTION BOOK

Bargains

Search for bargains in the day-old baked goods, dented can, and meat-that-is-about-to-expire bins. You have to be careful, but as long as the cans are not bulging or leaking and the appearance and dates meet your approval, go for it. Also look for generic and off-brands for additional savings.

Blanching

Serve vegetables that are bright green and crisp: Plunge them into 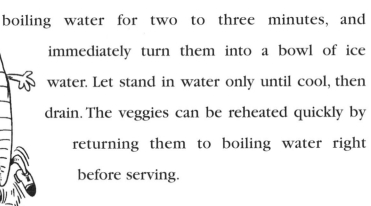 boiling water for two to three minutes, and immediately turn them into a bowl of ice water. Let stand in water only until cool, then drain. The veggies can be reheated quickly by returning them to boiling water right before serving.

Boiling

To cook below-the-ground vegetables (such as potatoes, carrots, and turnips), place in cold water and bring to a boil. Add above-the-ground vegetables (corn, peas, and beans) to water that's already boiling.

Bread dough rising

To create the perfect environment for bread dough rising, bring two cups of water to a boil in a two-quart pot. Remove the pot from the heat, invert the pot's lid on the top of the pot, and lay a potholder on the inverted lid. Put the dough in a mixing bowl, balance the bowl on the potholder in the inverted lid, and cover with a dishtowel. The water releases its heat gradually and keeps the dough at an ideal "proofing" temperature.

Campground ice cream

Ingredients: one cup heavy cream, one cup milk, one egg beaten, one-half cup sugar, one teaspoon vanilla. Mix well and place in clean, one-pound coffee can. Cover and tape shut. Place into a three-pound can with one part rock salt and four parts crushed ice. Cover. Roll back and forth on picnic table for ten minutes. Uncover both cans and stir ice cream. Recover small can and tape shut. Return to large coffee can with the salt and ice and roll five minutes more. (Caution: Be sure to use an egg that is not cracked, and thoroughly clean the shell before cracking it open.)

Cappuccino

To make four cappuccinos, pour two cups of milk into a glass measuring cup. Microwave on high until hot—about two minutes and twenty seconds. Place hot milk and one tablespoon of sugar in a blender. Cover with a vented lid and blend until frothy—about one minute. To serve, divide two cups strong coffee among four cups. Top each with frothy milk. Sprinkle with cinnamon or grated chocolate (optional).

How many chickens are in a cup? A three to four-pound broiler-fryer will yield three to four cups of cooked chicken, after deboning. A three-forths-pound skinned, deboned chicken breast will yield about two cups of cooked chicken.

Cooking vegetables

Add one-half to one teaspoon sugar to cooked vegetables such as carrots, corn, and peas. This reduces the starchy flavors and highlights natural sweetness. Brighten the flavor of frozen or canned peas, carrots, green beans, broccoli, or cauliflower by dropping a piece of lemon rind into the cooking water.

The date stamped on dairy products is the date when retailers must pull unsold products from the shelf. Properly stored, the product will be good for at least seven days past the printed date. Unsalted butter has a shorter shelf life than salted. Whichever kind you buy, extra sticks are best stored in the freezer. Milk, cream, cottage cheese, and similar products should be stored in their original containers. Also, to prolong its shelf life, store cottage cheese upside down.

Degrease stew

To degrease cooled meat soups and stews, put a sheet of waxed paper or plastic wrap directly on top of the liquid before refrigerating. When you're ready to reheat, peel off the paper or wrap, and the fat will come with it.

Discontinued products

Today's grocery stores will only carry those items that sell quickly in order to maintain their profit margin. Watch for product shelf labels with either a line drawn through the price code numbers or the letters *DC* or *Discontinued* written on them. By purchasing these "unadvertised" specials, you will often find savings of at least 20 percent or more on your register tape.

Eggs

If you have more eggs than you can use in the near future, crack them open and place them individually in an ice-cube tray. When the eggs are completely frozen, transfer the "cubes" to a freezer bag for future use. Frozen eggs should always be thawed in the refrigerator and used for recipes where they will be thoroughly cooked.

Eggs, easy peel

Eggs can be shelled easily if you bring them to a boil in a covered pan; then turn the heat to low and simmer for fifteen minutes. Pour off the hot water, shake the eggs in the pan until they're well cracked, then add cold water. Now, the shells should peel right off.

Ice cream

Store ice cream in the freezer compartment, not in the freezer door. This keeps it fresher because it is not exposed to sudden changes of temperature when the door is opened.

When baking, you can cut down or eliminate the use of butter or margarine by substituting applesauce. A good rule of thumb is no more than one tablespoon of applesauce per one cup of flour.

Marinade

For fast and easy marinating, all you need is a zippered storage bag and a straw. Mix the marinade in the bag, add the food, and zip the bag, leaving one corner open. Insert about one-half inch of the straw into the bag, and gently inhale on the straw. You will create a vacuum, causing the marinade to draw up around the food. When the marinade nears the top, quickly pull out the straw and seal the bag. You'll need less marinade, use less space in your refrigerator, and have less to clean up.

When buying meat, bear in mind that an expensive lean cut may be more economical than one that requires you to throw away excess bone, gristle, or fat.

Milk

To keep milk fresh longer, add a pinch of salt when it is first opened. This will greatly increase its useful shelf life and does not affect the taste in any way.

Muffins

When it's too hot to crank up the oven for an hour, bake your favorite quick bread in muffin pans rather than loaves. This cuts the baking time to a total of fifteen or twenty minutes and still allows for a great take-along to summertime picnics and potlucks.

One-pound equivalents

The following amounts are equal to one pound: two cups butter; two and one-third cups white granulated sugar; two cups packed brown sugar; four cups confectioners' sugar; three and a half cups all-purpose flour; four cups cake flour; three and three forths cups whole-wheat flour; four cups cocoa; three cups loosely packed raisins; two and three-forths cups sliced apples; two cups fresh, pitted cherries; five cups sliced, fresh mushrooms; three cups sliced white potatoes; four and a half cups coarsely sliced cabbage.

Pasta shapes

Match the pasta shape to the sauce you will be serving. Serve long, thin pasta like spaghetti or vermicelli with smooth sauces that will cling to the long strands better than chunky vegetable and meat sauces. Serve long, flat pasta like fettuccini and linguini with rich sauces based on butter, cheese, or cream. Serve short pasta like fusilli or rigatoni with chunky vegetable, meat, or cream sauces (good choice for baked pasta dishes). Serve fun-shaped pasta like bow ties or shells with cream, seafood, or tomato sauce.

Pick a fish

For best quality, buy from supermarkets that display fish on ice in refrigerated cases. A freshly caught fish has almost no odor; it will not smell "fishy." An ammonia-like smell develops when fish has been stored several days. Don't buy! The eyes should look clear, (not cloudy); the scales should be bright pink (not gray). The flesh should be unblemished, with its edges intact (not torn); when pressed with a finger, the flesh should give slightly but bounce back.

Piecrust

To prevent piecrust edges from over browning, cut the bottom and sides from a disposable aluminum foil pie pan, leaving the rim intact. When the crust is light golden brown but the filling isn't quite done, place the foil ring around the crust edge to slow the browning process. This rim can be used again and again.

Punch cubes

In ice-cube trays, freeze ahead of time whatever drink you will be serving. For example, if serving tea, make tea cubes; if punch, punch cubes. This way drinks will stay chilled without getting all watered down.

Salad greens

Prevent soggy greens and still prepare the salad ahead of time: Place the dressing in the bottom of the bowl. Add cucumbers and other ingredients that marinate well. Then add the greens. Cover with a damp towel and refrigerate. Toss just before serving.

Salty soup

If you've added too much salt to the soup, don't panic. Simply cut up a raw potato and allow it to cook in the soup for a while. It will absorb the excess salt. Then simply remove potato before serving.

Single portions

To freeze single-sized portions if you don't have many small containers or have limited freezer space, spoon the desired amount of food, such as chili or stew, into a large container; freeze briefly until firm; cover with two pieces of waxed paper; then add another serving. Repeat layers with remaining food. When ready to use, just grab the edges of the waxed paper, lift out what you need, and return the rest to the freezer.

Steaming vegetables

Put fresh vegetables in a resealable plastic bag, add a bit of water, and seal the bag; but leave a small opening for steam to escape. Place in the microwave and cook for two to three minutes, or until tender.

For a delicious and festive roast turkey, insert sprigs of fresh herbs in a single layer between the skin and breast meat, arranging them in a decorative pattern. Then roast the turkey as usual. The herbs will flavor the meat and show through the skin in an attractive design.

HOME

CHEAPSKATE'S LITTLE INSTRUCTION BOOK

Air-conditioner filter

To clean an air-conditioner or humidifier filter, take the foam filter out of the grill and soak it in a solution of equal parts of white vinegar and warm water. If you clean the filter regularly, an hour of soaking will be plenty. Simply squeeze the filter dry when it's clean and place it back into the air conditioner.

Aluminum cookware

To remove stains and coloration from aluminum cookware, fill the cookware with hot water and add two tablespoons cream of tartar for each quart of water. Bring the solution to a boil, and simmer for ten minutes. Wash as usual and dry.

Art gallery

If you enjoy decorating your home or apartment with framed art prints, discover a wonderful resource offered by many public libraries. Some carry hundreds of framed art prints that library patrons may check out free of charge for a specified time period of two or even three months. Designate a particular wall in your home as your "revolving art gallery," where you enjoy a broad range of artistic styles at no cost to you.

Ashes

Ashes from a wood-burning stove or fireplace make wonderful fertilizer for rose bushes and other prizes in your yard and garden. Collect the ashes and scatter them around shrubs and bushes. Ashes enrich the soil's texture and will produce a greener garden. Fireplace ashes act like lime in the garden, making your soil more alkaline. (If your soil is already alkaline, don't use them.) A gallon of dry ashes equals about three pounds; and if used as a soil additive, apply at the rate of five pounds per hundred square feet.

Household cleaner

Dissolve four tablespoons baking soda in one quart of warm water for a basic bathroom cleaner. Use dry baking soda on a damp sponge for tough areas. Baking soda will clean and deodorize all kitchen and bathroom surfaces.

Beach bag

Along with your regular beach paraphernalia, throw in a large zippered storage bag with a quarter cup of baking soda added inside. Use this to bring home wet bathing suits. Just put them in the bag and shake it. The soda absorbs moisture, helping to prevent mildew and scary smells until you can get the suits properly laundered.

Bleached-out rug spots

Color in bleached-out spots in your carpeting (bleaching often occurs near a bathroom where cleaning products have splashed or dripped). Use a non-toxic marking pen in a shade as close as you can find to that of the rug. This is exactly what a carpet professional would do if you called for repair.

Blender

To clean the blender, fill it less than half way with hot, soapy water; replace the lid, and turn the machine on at the lowest speed for a minute or two. Rinse the blender thoroughly; then towel dry it before storing.

Blood stains

Presoak bloodstained fabric in cold water for at least thirty minutes. If the stain remains, soak in lukewarm ammonia water (three tablespoons ammonia per gallon of water), and rinse. If the stain still remains, work in the detergent and wash, using fabric-safe bleach.

Brilliantly white

If you want to keep your white laundry stain-free and brilliantly white without using chlorine bleach, here's the secret: Fill the washing machine with the hottest water available. Add one cup Cascade™ automatic dishwasher powder and one cup washing soda (located in the supermarket laundry section). Add washable whites and allow machine to agitate for a few minutes. Turn the machine off and soak whites at least three hours (overnight is fine). Finish the cycle and dry as usual.

Carpet bargain

If you are not in a big hurry and are fairly flexible as to color and quality, let the carpet stores in your area that offer "Complete Satisfaction Guaranteed" know that you would be interested in purchasing the carpeting someone else has rejected. Many times when new carpet is installed, the homeowner for one reason or another is not completely satisfied with some aspect of the carpet and takes advantage of the carpet supplier's satisfaction guarantee. You should be able to make a real bargain on the like-new goods, including installation.

Carpet stains

A highly effective and economical way to remove stains from carpeting is to mix together one part Tide™ powder laundry detergent, two parts white vinegar, and two parts warm water. Scrub soiled area; then rinse with clear, warm water. From oil to mud to wine stains, they'll all disappear.

Ceramic tile floors

Mop ceramic tile floors with a solution of one gallon hot water and one cup vinegar. Don't use any soap. The floor will shine and sparkle like new with no rinsing required. While hot water might work to remove dirt, it will have a dulling effect because of the minerals left behind in the water. Vinegar however, cuts and removes those minerals, getting rid of that cloudy film.

Citrus insect repellent

To prevent ants, spiders, and bugs from entering your home or another structure, spray the foundation and the grout within a foot of the wall with a mixture of one-half cup ground lemon (you can puree the lemon in a blender or food processor), including the rind, and one gallon of water. Apply with a garden sprinkling can. Not only is the weak solution versatile, it's mild, inexpensive, and environmentally sound.

Wallpaper stains

Remove those ugly stains without harming even your most delicate wallpaper: First, blot the wallpaper with talcum powder to absorb the stain. Then wash with warm, soapy water (for grease stains add white vinegar).

Dishwasher soap extender

This solution will extend your favorite brand of automatic dishwasher soap by 50 percent and also prevent spotting. Mix one cup borax and one-half cup baking soda with three cups of your favorite dishwasher detergent. Store in a clean, tightly closed container. Use this in the same quantity as straight dishwasher detergent. (Caution: If you have a home water-softening unit, do not use this formula. It will react with the chemicals in your water and could permanently etch fine glassware.)

Dishwasher spots

No matter which dishwasher detergent you use, glasses often come out with spots. Solution: Mix equal parts water, vinegar, and lemon juice in a spray bottle and spray the glasses before putting them in the washer. No spots!

Disinfecting

To disinfect a wood chopping block that can harbor harmful bacteria, mix a solution of three tablespoons of bleach to one quart of water and pour it over the wood. Wait a few minutes before rinsing well. This also works with a plastic cutting board.

Drain maintenance

To clear a sluggish drain, pour one cup baking soda into the drain followed by one cup white vinegar. Allow to sit overnight. In the morning, flush with a kettle full of boiling water. Plunge the drain a few times with a plunger. This is an excellent maintenance tactic to keep drains running well.

Dryer sheets

Save the dryer sheets from your laundry after they've softened a load of wash. They make great dusting and cleaning cloths for television and computer screens. Not only will they clean the screens, the antistatic properties will treat the screens to repel, rather than attract, dust.

Exchange instead of sell

Tired of selling a big-ticket item at a garage sale and not ending up with enough money to replace it with the needed larger size? Don't. Instead, organize a neighborhood exchange for things like old rollerblades, party shoes, and bicycles the kids have outgrown. You'll be surprised to find out how many of your neighbors are in the same boat.

Fertilizer: One cent a gallon

Here's a great way to brew up your own plant fertilizer at a cost of about one cent per gallon: Add two teaspoons of plain household ammonia to one gallon of water. Allow to sit for a full twenty-four hours. Use on plants instead of costly commercial fertilizer. (Caution: If you use more than a capful to one gallon of water, the solution will be too strong, and you will burn your plants. In this case, less is definitely better.)

Firewood in the bag

When gathering kindling or pieces of wood from outdoors for the fireplace, carry them into the house in a brown grocery bag. Place the entire bag and contents into the fireplace and light the bag. This prevents that inevitable trail of wood, dirt, and debris that always follows the person carrying wood into the house, and it's a tidy way to start a fire.

Fluorescent lightbulbs

Replace incandescent lightbulbs with fluorescent ones. The initial cost of fluorescents is quite a bit more, but they use a quarter of the energy and last ten to fifteen times longer than their incandescent counterparts. If you can't make the switch all at once, make it gradually—one or two bulbs a month—until all have been replaced.

Frozen policies

Do not keep wills or life insurance policies in a safe-deposit box. It is not unusual for a safe-deposit box to be sealed at the time of death, making it difficult for the survivors. Instead, keep these important documents in a fireproof safe, or wrap them in plastic and put them in a sealed container in the freezer. They will be easily accessible and protected in case of fire.

Furnace filter restoration

Instead of replacing your furnace filter every month or as recommended by the manufacturer, vacuum it, and spray the cleaned filter with Endust™. This will restore the dust-catching ability of the recycled filter, allowing it to continue working effectively for three additional periods before it should be replaced.

Garbage disposal

To clean the garbage disposal, dump in a tray of ice cubes made from white vinegar and water. Turn on the water and operate the disposal as usual. Or dump in a tray of regular ice cubes and a handful of lemon rinds and operate the disposal as usual.

Garden tools

Keep a bucket of sand sprinkled lightly with mineral oil in the shed or garage where you store your garden tools. When you're done using the tools, scour them with a bit of the sand to keep them clean and rust-free. The oil will leave a light protective coating on the blades to prevent rust.

Green air cleaners

The world's best home air fresheners are green plants. Houseplants help filter the air of indoor pollutants, like formaldehyde and benzene. The best of these green air cleaners are spider plants, philodendron, and aloe vera. Work plants into your home's environment whenever you can. One plant for about every hundred square feet can remove up to 87 percent of toxic organic pollutants. And their gift to the home? They produce oxygen.

Hang a picture

This is the formula that professional picture hangers use: (1) Measure up sixty inches from the floor. (2) To this, add half the height of the framed picture. (3) Subtract the height of the wire (the height of the triangle that the wire would form if the frames were actually hanging in place). This magic number is the distance from the floor at which you should nail the picture hook, regardless of the height of the ceiling or even your height.

Indentations in carpet

Here is how to make those carpet indentations rebound: Place an ice cube in each indentation. Let it melt; then wait about twelve hours before blotting up the moisture. Gently pull up the carpet fibers using a kitchen fork.

Ink remover

Place the ink-stained fabric over several thicknesses of paper towels. In a small bowl, combine one tablespoon white vinegar, one tablespoon milk, one teaspoon lemon juice, and one teaspoon borax, and "paint" the ink spot. Wait for a few minutes, and then sponge the area with cool water. Repeat until the stain is gone.

Jewelry cleaner

Here's the fine-jewelry cleaner professional stores use: Mix equal amounts of household ammonia and water. Drop jewelry into a small container of this cleaner. Allow to sit for a few minutes; then brush with an old toothbrush. Rinse well in clear water. It's inexpensive and it works. (Caution: Never use this solution on opals, pearls, or other soft stones.)

Laminate surfaces

Applying a coat of a good automobile wax can brighten plastic laminate countertops that have become dull with age. Allow the wax to dry slightly and buff off. This also will make the surface stain- and scratch-resistant. None of the wax will remain except the shine, so it's perfectly safe to put food on the counter afterward.

Wash all but the most soiled clothes in warm or even cold water, followed by a cold rinse. According to the Department of Energy, this saves the average family fifty dollars a year without affecting the quality of the wash.

Wick while away

If you must leave small potted plants unattended while on vacation, push a needle threaded with wool yarn into the soil, and put the other end in a jar of water. The plants will stay moist through this wicking system.

Here's how to find water leaks in your house: Turn off all running water in the house. Find your water meter and take a look. Is it still moving? Chances are you have a water leak, and chances are even better it's your toilet. Put a few drops of food coloring into the toilet tank. If without flushing, the color shows up in the bowl, it's definitely leaking. Get a toilet repair kit at the home repair center. This is a simple do-it-yourself repair.

Liquid hand soap

Grate lots of soap slivers with a cheese grater, mix with water (the amount depends on how much soap you have, but generally speaking you want about one part grated soap to three parts water), and melt in microwave or on the stove. Beat with a rotary beater until smooth. If you don't want to bother with slivers but want to make your own liquid soap, follow these instructions using a full bar of soap and three cups of water.

Metal furniture

To clean aluminum, steel, or wrought-iron furniture, wash with a mild liquid detergent and water, then rinse and dry thoroughly. Once a season, apply a coat of automobile wax. If a scratch occurs on wrought iron or steel, apply matching exterior paint with a small artist's brush.

Microwave cleaning

To zap microwave odors and steam clean the interior, place two cups of water with two tablespoons lemon juice in a microwavable bowl. Heat in the microwave on high for twelve to fifteen minutes. The mixture will bubble, boil, and steam. Carefully remove the bowl and wipe the interior with a clean sponge.

Here's a way to get rid of mildew buildup in your shower stall without using harsh, household bleach: Fill an empty spray bottle with vinegar and a cup of salt. Spray the stall, allow the solution to sit for at least a half hour, and then rinse thoroughly. Tougher jobs may require a second application.

Monthly maintenance

Take care of your washing machine, and you'll add years to its useful life. To unclog hoses and flush out all the minerals and gummy buildup, fill the machine with hot water, pour in a gallon of distilled white vinegar, and allow it to run through an entire cycle.

Natural insect repellent

Pots of sweet basil placed strategically around the patio, swimming pool, or doorway repel flies. Crush bay leaves between your fingers; then rub your fingers over your skin to repel gnats, flies, and even mosquitoes.

Paint storage

Store partially filled cans of paint upside down. The paint will form an airtight seal, extending its useful life.

Photocopy wallet contents

Make a photocopy of everything in your wallet. Now if you lose it or it's stolen, you'll have a record of the important information and can move quickly to have things replaced or canceled.

Propane

Never sure how much propane is left in the barbecue tank? Make a streak down the side with a wet sponge. Moisture will evaporate more quickly from the upper, empty portion.

If your kitchen or bathroom is suffering from outdated avocado green or some other ugly colored ceramic tile, and you don't want to replace it, do this: Purchase a product like Fleckstone™ (manufactured by Plasti-kote™), available at home improvement centers. It is a multi-hued, textured spray paint sold together with a clear acrylic topcoat that, when applied as directed, produces "new" tile that can be cleaned with a damp sponge. Even if it takes five kits to do the job, you'll spend around fifty dollars, and that sure beats the cost of remodeling.

Remove that hemline

To remove the permanent press line from a hem that has been let down, dampen the crease with white vinegar and press with a piece of aluminum foil between the material and iron.

Shiny plant leaves

Apply a thin coat of petroleum jelly to the top surface of smooth houseplant leaves for instant shine. However, leave the underside of the leaf alone, because that's how plants breathe. You don't want to smother your philodendron!

Shower curtain with mildew

To clean mildew and soap scum from a shower curtain, place the curtain in the washing machine along with two or three white towels. Fill with warm water; add detergent, and one-half cup baking soda. Add one cup white vinegar to the rinse water to prevent further mold from forming. Hang on the shower rod to dry.

Sink-stopper leaks

To stop water from leaking out of the kitchen sink while you're doing dishes, put a piece of plastic wrap between the drain and the drain stopper. This is also a handy trick to remember if you're soaking something overnight.

Snails and slugs

To keep snails and slugs out of your garden, sink pie pans into the garden so that the rims are flush with the ground. Fill with beer. The slugs and snails will be attracted to the beer, which will be their final undoing. (This is a lovely object lesson for kids who think it's cool to drink beer!) Simply empty the pie pans when they're full of dead snails and slugs.

Spot remover for wool and silk

An excellent spot remover for wool and silk is Murphy's Oil Soap™ (available in the household cleaning section of the supermarket). Use directly on the fabric and allow it to soak in. Wash as usual. Always test on an inconspicuous area first, like an inside seam. Murphy's™ is also great for cars, floors, wood furniture, and cabinets.

Stained woodwork

To clean painted woodwork stained by grease and smoke, dissolve old-fashioned, dry laundry starch in water according to the package directions. Paint it on the stain, and when it dries, rub the area with a soft brush or clean cloth. This removes the stains without harming the finish.

Stud finding

Studs are the vertical wooden supports behind your walls. They're handy for hanging pictures, because a nail or screw is more likely to stay in place when it's been driven into a stud (as opposed to just the drywall). Locate studs behind a wall by finding the electrical outlet (which is attached to one side of a stud), and measure sixteen inches in either direction to find the next stud. (Note: Some new homes have studs twenty-four inches on center.)

Thrift store instead

If your garage sale merchandise is mainly old clothes in not-so-great condition, consider a trip to the thrift shop instead. At a tax benefit of ten dollars or more per bag of clothes, this tactic may possibly be more lucrative in the long run.

Tight lids

When you can't remove a too-tight lid from a jar, this handy hint may do the trick: Take a heavy-duty rubber band, put it around the lid, and twist. Because the rubber band gives you something to grip, the lid should come off easily.

Toilet

To remove stubborn hard-water deposits from a toilet bowl, first remove as much water from the bowl as possible by either plunging it out or pouring a big bucket of water into the bowl. Heat a gallon of white vinegar to boiling, and carefully pour it into the almost-empty toilet bowl. Allow it to stand for a few hours or until completely cool. Then scrub with a brush and flush to clear.

Unlisted phone number fee

Don't pay a monthly fee to have an unlisted phone number, also called a nonpublished number in some areas. The fee for unlisted service costs anywhere from one dollar to five dollars a month. If for security and privacy reasons you can't let your name be published, use your pet's name, the middle name of one of your children, or your maiden name instead. Your security will not be compromised, because if someone calls for your pet, you'll know immediately that it is probably not someone with whom you care to speak.

Wallpaper removal

To remove wallpaper, mix equal parts white vinegar and hot water. Dip a paint roller into the solution, and apply until the paper is thoroughly wet. After two applications, most paper will peel off in sheets. Patience is the secret.

Washcloths

The next time you see cotton bath towels on sale, buy one and give this a try: Cut it into eight washcloths. Either serge the edges or use a zigzag or overlock stitch on a regular sewing machine. You should be able to make loads of wonderful washcloths for a fraction of the cost of ready-made ones.

Water heater maintenance

Perform water heater maintenance twice yearly, and you'll get many more years of service from it. Turn off the power to the water heater at the circuit breaker and drain the sediment from the bottom of the tank before refilling.

Waxed produce

Some vegetables, such as bell peppers and cucumbers, are coated with wax before they're shipped to the store. Waxing is done to extend shelf life, seal in moisture, and improve appearance. The waxes are safe to eat but may contain pesticide residue, so carefully wash all waxed vegetables and fruit.

Weed killer

Here's a great weed killer you can make for less than two dollars a gallon. Dissolve one pound table salt in a gallon of white vinegar (5 percent acidity is ideal). Add eight drops of liquid dishwashing detergent (helps plant material absorb the liquid). Label and keep out of reach of children. Use in an ordinary spray bottle. This non-toxic formulation acts as a temporary soil sterilizer, so don't spray near roots of trees, shrubs, or plants you'd like to keep. It is especially effective on gravel driveways.

White appliance touch-up

The nasty black chip on any white home appliance, porcelain sink, ceramic tile, or even your white car can be quickly repaired with a liquid correction fluid like White-Out™ or Liquid Paper™, available at office supply stores. Carefully paint the chip, and it will dry in just a few minutes.

Whiteflies, spider mites, mealybugs, cinch bugs, and aphids

To kill these little pests, mix well three tablespoons liquid Ivory™ soap in a gallon of water. Fill a sprayer with the soapy solution and mist the leaves of plants and bushes.

Window screens, cleaning

First, run a dry sponge over the screen to remove any loose dust. Next, with the screen propped at a slight angle against a tree or wall, pour a solution of sudsy ammonia and water (one cup to one gallon) across the top. When it starts to dribble down, rub with a scrub brush, using an up-and-down motion. Repeat this procedure on side two. Then rinse the screen with a garden hose and place it in the sun to dry.

Window screens, patch

To repair a small tear in a window screen, cut a square patch a little larger than the damaged area. (You can buy screening at the hardware store.) Unravel and remove a few strands of wire from all four sides. Bend the wire ends over till you can slip them through the screen. Then bend them farther to hold the patch in place.

Wrinkle-free

Throw wrinkled clothes into the dryer, along with a damp towel or washcloth. Turn the dryer on; and in the time it takes you to get ready, all the wrinkles will iron themselves away. This tip works especially well for clothes left in the dryer overnight.

MONEY &
FINANCE

CHEAPSKATE'S LITTLE INSTRUCTION BOOK

Credit card application disposal

If you are not interested in a pre-approved credit application you receive in the mail (tell me you're not), don't throw it in the trash. A thief who finds it can actually take out an account in your name, using another address, and begin making charges. Always destroy applications by cutting them into bits and disposing of the pieces in two or three different trash receptacles. Because thieves are really clever these days, your goal should be to make it impossible for them to put the paperwork back together.

Credit unions

Want low- or no-fee checking accounts and perhaps free checks also? Then see if there is any way you can qualify to join a credit union. Most welcome spouses, children, brothers, sisters, and parents of the member. As a member, you will enjoy many benefits: federally insured deposits, low-interest auto loans, and higher earnings than bank interest rates on your savings accounts.

Increase the deductible on your auto insurance and save collision insurance. For example, if your insurance policy currently provides a two hundred dollar deductible, meaning you will be required to pay the first two hundred dollars of any claim, increase it to five hundred dollars; and your premiums will drop dramatically. Call your insurance agent to obtain quotes on various deductible amounts—just be sure you are able to come up with the deductible, no matter the amount, if you ever do have to file a claim. In fact, you'd be wise to have an amount equal to your deductible stashed in an interest-bearing account just in case, and then drive defensively to reduce the risk of having to use it.

Guidelines for beginning investors

As a beginning investor, any plan you consider should have all of the following features, or you will run a great risk of failure: (1) The investment must be simple to understand and easy to follow. (2) It must take very little time to administrate. (3) It should not cause you stress or anxiety. (4) It must not change your lifestyle or cause disharmony in your home. (5) You must be able to handle the investment entirely on your own. (6) It must have the advantage of liquidity (getting your money back quickly in the event of an emergency). (7) It must work equally well for the person with little to invest as well as the wealthy investor.

Call the Social Security Administration at 800-772-1213 for a "Request of Earnings and Benefits Estimate Statement." After you mail back the completed form, you will receive a statement showing all the money you have paid into Social Security, as well as a personalized estimated monthly benefit upon retirement. If there are mistakes, such as not being credited for the correct number of years or an erroneous statement of earnings, the record can be corrected, but only if you report it. You'll be happy to know that the Social Security Administration has recently begun sending this statement out on an annual basis.

Layaway

Most stores offer layaway plans. This is a great way to purchase something over a period of time without incurring debt. As long as the store holds the merchandise until you make all of the payments, it is not a debt. This also means you are free to change your mind and obtain a refund if you so desire. In a sense, layaway forces you to save for things before you purchase them.

Mortgage insurance

Typically overpriced, mortgage insurance, (not to be confused with private mortgage insurance [PMI], which is completely different) like life insurance, pays off your remaining mortgage balance in the case of your demise. But who says your spouse or heirs would want to apply insurance proceeds to pay off the mortgage, which may be the lowest interest debt you leave them? If you have this type of coverage, they'll have no choice. It is far better to buy regular term insurance. It's much less expensive and leaves your heirs with more options.

Mortgage interest rate

Inquire if the financial institution servicing your mortgage offers an interest rate reduction when payments are automatically paid from your checking account. Example: A credit union recently introduced a .25 percent reduction for any member who authorizes automatic withdrawal.

Scanners

Many retail stores that are equipped with checkout scanners have store policies that say you get the item free if the price is scanned incorrectly. Stay alert and watch the prices that are scanned. If you see something that doesn't look right, speak up. Curiously, each year overall scanner errors in this country register in the millions of dollars to the benefit of the retailer.

Start saving for the future

Regardless of how much debt you have or how little money you make, saving some amount consistently in a special place or account is going to change your attitude. Saving even a few dollars each week helps fill the emptiness that drives some of us to spend. Remember, something of everything you earn is yours to keep.

Warranties

Find a large three-ring binder and a supply of plastic pocket inserts. Whenever you purchase a product, whether it's an appliance, lawn tool, or toy, staple the receipt to the owner's manual or warranty paperwork and file it away in one of the pockets. Now whenever something stops working or has a problem, you'll have the paperwork and all the information at your fingertips, including the customer service number. Always call—even if the warranty is expired. Explain the situation and your purchase details, and then ask one simple question: "What can you do for me?"

TRAVEL &
AUTOMOBILES

CHEAPSKATE'S LITTLE INSTRUCTION BOOK

Have your brakes replaced before the rotors have to be turned. You'll save hundreds of dollars. It should not cost you anything for your mechanic to check and tell you how much of the pad is remaining. Don't push it past 5 percent.

Buyer's guide sticker

If you are considering buying a used car from a dealer, become familiar with the buyer's guide sticker posted on every used car offered for sale (for-sale-by-owner cars excluded). It was originated by the Federal Trade Commission as a consumer protection device. Before you start shopping, read the FTC pamphlet that explains the buyer's guide. Send fifty cents to: Consumer Information Center-F, P.O. Box 100, Pueblo, CO 81002, and request publication 440T "BUYING A USED CAR."

Cheaper flights

An airline flight that makes a stop between your departure city and your destination can sometimes cost significantly less than one that makes no stops. You may have to spend an extra hour or two on the ground and risk additional delays, but the savings may be worth it.

The Complete Car Cost Guide

The best single resource for determining what it will cost to own a particular vehicle is *The Complete Car Cost Guide*, about forty-five dollars, available from Intelli Choice, Inc., 800-227-2665. This book evaluates depreciation, gas consumption, insurance costs, and frequency of repairs to derive the average five-year cost of operating each car.

Fill up early in the day

Fuel your gas tank early in the morning, and you'll get 5 percent more gas for the same price. The heat of the afternoon sun causes gasoline to expand in the station's fuel tank so less pumps out as the day wears on. The average early bird will save up to fifty dollars a year on fuel.

Floor mats to the rescue

If your car gets stuck in the snow, slip one or more of the floor mats under the stuck tire(s) to provide the traction you need to get out. Don't forget to run back and retrieve your mats, unless to do so would place you and your passengers in harm's way.

Don't carry more than you need. A light load gets much better gas mileage. Clean out heavy items from the trunk, and leave only the spare tire and safety equipment. Don't make your car a mobile warehouse for things you can just as easily store in the garage.

Leaks in the suitcase

Make sure the bottles of shampoo, lotions, and makeup in your suitcase don't leak all over your clothes. Put a bit of cotton inside each bottle cap before closing it. Then place your bottles in plastic zippered storage bags for extra protection.

Overheating first aid

At the first sign of your car engine overheating, shut off the air conditioner and open the windows to decrease the load on the motor and help it cool down. If the car is still overheating, turn on the heater and blower to transfer the heat from the engine to the interior. If you are stopped in traffic, shift into neutral and rev the engine a little to speed up the water pump and fan. The increased circulation should help cool things off.

Priority handling

Attach to your luggage bright, neon-colored tags that have been printed with the word "Priority" and laminated at a local printing company. Your bags will attract the attention of baggage handlers and will usually be the first to come off the plane. As a bonus, your luggage will stand out in a sea of look-alike baggage.

Renting a car

If you rent a car, reject offers of additional optional coverage if you currently carry auto insurance on the car(s) you own. Be prepared for some heavy-handed tactics to get you to accept it. Sales people get hefty bonuses if they can persuade you. Be sure to call your insurance agent to check on rental car coverage, though, ahead of time.

Save on hotel rates

On any given day, hotels can have many different rates, depending on occupancy. Always call the hotel desk instead of the toll-free reservation number. Ask about weekend rates, holiday and seasonal specials, or discounts for affiliations you might have, such as the Automobile Club of America.

Secret warranties

Some automakers issue special warranties on certain aspects of the auto that are kept quiet and secret from the automobile owner. To find out if your car has secret warranties, send the year, make, and model along with a large self-addressed, stamped envelope to the Center for Auto Safety, 2001 S. Street N.W., Washington, D.C. 20009. They will respond with a description of all secret warranties on your car.

Travel ready

To keep everything organized when you pack for a trip, group all the small essentials into large, plastic, zippered storage bags. When you get to the hotel, put your bedside bag (travel alarm clock, flashlight, and nightlight) on the night table, and the toiletries bag (powder, deodorant, toothbrush, hair essentials, and makeup) on the bathroom shelf. Everything's together, easy to use, ready to go in a moment's notice, and you probably won't find yourself leaving things behind.

Vinyl dashboard and upholstery

The greatest enemy of your car's vinyl dashboard and interior is the sun's heat and ultraviolet rays. Here's what you can do to slow down vinyl deterioration: First clean the vinyl upholstery and dashboard. Dry well and apply sunscreen lotion with the highest UV factor you can find—just rub it in as you would on your skin. When the sunscreen has had time to soak in, buff off any excess and apply a commercial vinyl protectant, which will help seal it.

About the Author

Mary Hunt, a reformed credit card junkie and America's favorite cheapskate, is founder, editor, and publisher of *Cheapskate Monthly*, a national subscription newsletter that promotes financially responsible, debt-free living. She also is the author of six books, including *Tiptionary* (Broadman & Holman Publishers, 1997) from which she gleaned her best insights to compile this handy money and timesaving guide. Her appearances include spots on *Good Morning America*, *The Oprah Winfrey Show*, *The Hour of Power*, and *Focus on the Family*.

To subscribe to *Cheapskate Monthly*, send check or money order for $18 to:

Cheapskate Monthly
P.O. Box 2135
Paramount, CA 90723-8135

(562) 630-8845 or (562) 630-6474

Additional copies of this book
are available from your local bookstore.

If you have enjoyed this book, or if it has
impacted your life, we would like to hear from you.
Please contact us at:

Trade Life Publishers
Department E
P.O. Box 55325
Tulsa, Oklahoma 74155